T0067846

WHO TOLD YOU, YOU COULDN'T DO THAT?

When God Told You, You Can!

31 Day Devotional and Journal for Relentless Faith

JENNIFER N. HARRIS

WESTBOW
PRESS®
A DIVISION OF THOMAS NELSON
& ZONDERVAN

Copyright © 2019 Jennifer N. Harris.

All rights reserved. No part of this book may be used or reproduced by any means, graphic, electronic, or mechanical, including photocopying, recording, taping or by any information storage retrieval system without the written permission of the author except in the case of brief quotations embodied in critical articles and reviews.

This book is a work of non-fiction. Unless otherwise noted, the author and the publisher make no explicit guarantees as to the accuracy of the information contained in this book and in some cases, names of people and places have been altered to protect their privacy.

WestBow Press books may be ordered through booksellers or by contacting:

WestBow Press
A Division of Thomas Nelson & Zondervan
1663 Liberty Drive
Bloomington, IN 47403
www.westbowpress.com
844-714-3454

Because of the dynamic nature of the Internet, any web addresses or links contained in this book may have changed since publication and may no longer be valid. The views expressed in this work are solely those of the author and do not necessarily reflect the views of the publisher, and the publisher hereby disclaims any responsibility for them.

Any people depicted in stock imagery provided by Getty Images are models, and such images are being used for illustrative purposes only. Certain stock imagery © Getty Images.

ISBN: 978-1-9736-4371-5 (sc)
ISBN: 978-1-9736-4373-9 (hc)
ISBN: 978-1-9736-4372-2 (e)

Library of Congress Control Number: 2018912792

Print information available on the last page.

WestBow Press rev. date: 05/14/2019

Unless noted otherwise, all Scripture quotations are
taken from the King James Version.

Scripture quotations marked NKJV are taken from the New King James Version®.
Copyright © 1982 by Thomas Nelson. Used by permission. All rights reserved.

Scripture quotations marked NIV are taken from The Holy Bible, New
International Version®, NIV® Copyright © 1973, 1978, 1984, 2011 by
Biblica, Inc.® Used by permission. All rights reserved worldwide.

Scripture quotations marked GNT are taken from the Good News
Translation® (Today's English Version, Second Edition). Copyright
© 1992 American Bible Society. All rights reserved.

Scripture quotations marked MSG are taken from The Message. Copyright © 1993,
1994, 1995, 1996, 2000, 2001, 2002. Used by permission of NavPress Publishing Group.

Scripture quotations marked ESV taken from The Holy Bible, English
Standard Version® (ESV®), Copyright © 2001 by Crossway, a
publishing ministry of Good News Publishers. All rights reserved.

Scripture quotations marked DRB are taken from the Douay Rheims Bible.

Scripture quotations marked NASB are taken from The New American
Standard Bible®, Copyright © 1960, 1962, 1963, 1968, 1971, 1972, 1973,
1975, 1977, 1995 by The Lockman Foundation. Used by permission.

Scripture quotations marked NLT are taken from the Holy Bible,
New Living Translation, Copyright © 1996, 2004, 2015 by Tyndale
House Foundation. Used by permission of Tyndale House Publishers,
Inc., Carol Stream, Illinois 60188. All rights reserved.

DEDICATION

This book is dedicated to my late father DeWayne and my late sister Taryn, who always saw more in me, than I saw in myself, and reminded me to not sweat the small stuff, but use that energy to excel in life. I miss you both tremendously. You are not forgotten.

To my mother Claudia, and my daughter Essence, thank you for your love, support, and for all of your years of time and hard work. Thank you Essence for always being a bright ray of light.

To my husband Tyrone, thank you for your love and for reminding me to stay focused and get busy. I love all of you.

PREFACE

Who told you you can't, when God said you can? Life and death are in the power of the tongue, and It is crucial and essential to understand this sooner than later.

When you are surrounded by people who have a negative or condemning tongue, it can be easy to fall into the trap of speaking negatively, or seeing yourself as defeated, and unable to reach your dreams or goals. But regardless of what people say to you, or about you that is not in your favor, keep in mind, that if God Be for you, who can be against you.

The words we speak carry weight and have power, either to help you excel or to slow you down. The word of God is filled with numerous scriptures on the power of the tongue. In James 3:5-6 NIV It talks about how the the tongue has the capacity to set the whole course of one's life on fire. James goes on to say that the tongue is hard to tame, even calling the tongue, a fire. Which is why it is essential we use words to shape and accelerate, and not to destroy.

Ephesians 4:29 NIV talks about never allowing deceitful speech to leave our mouth, but only that which is helpful for building others up. Well, you can also use your speech to uplift and build your self up. We edify, encourage and motivate others but when it comes to ourselves, many times we fall short.

I myself have been guilty of that. Expecting and speaking the best over others, but at times failing to encourage myself. Once I began to alter my speech and my expectations, my faith increased and the course of my life began to improve.

This book is written for those who want to encourage others while uplifting and believing the same for themselves. No matter who told you its impossible, remember with God all things are possible, and you truly are more than a conqueror. Remember death and life are in the power of the tongue; and they that love it shall eat the fruit thereof (Proverbs 18:21 KJV). Let this book be a daily reminder.

DAY 1

Begin with Prayer

Rejoice always, pray without ceasing, give thanks in all circumstances; for this is the will of God in Christ Jesus for you. (1 Thessalonians 5:16-18 ESV)

Devotion

Prayer is defined as an earnest request, address or petition to God in word or thought. Prayer connects us to God. He expects us to use it to our fullest ability, praying without ceasing, and in the Spirit at all times. Everything we do, we need to begin with prayer. For every need or desire we have, we should be covering it in prayer. Prayer produces results, as we pray the will, and the word of God. It is written that when we pray, Angels hearken unto the voice of His word. Prayer is a powerful force that can silence and cripple the enemy and anything that is opposing you. You can bind that which is not of God, and begin to loose those things that are. You are not waiting on God. God is waiting on you. He will not do anything until you begin to pray.

Scriptures: Psalm 103:20 KJV; Ephesians 6:18 KJV

Prayer

Father, I submit myself unto you today, praying before I make any decisions. You direct my path, and order my steps. You know my beginning from my end, and I desire to be in your will. Today is the day the Lord has made, I shall rejoice and be glad in it. I bind every negative and destructive force that is opposing me and my livelihood, and I now loose and release the will and the promises of God in every area of my life. And because I am the righteousness of God in Christ Jesus, I thank you that my effectual fervent prayers have availed much. In Jesus' name, amen.

Scriptures: James 5:16 KJV

NOTES

NOTES

DAY 2

Pray According To His Will

Beloved, I wish above all things that thou mayest prosper and be in health, even as thy soul prospereth. (3 John 1:2 KJV)

Devotion

Success, prosperity, and divine health, these are all things that God desires for you. That's right! Above all things he wants you to be successful in every area of your life. Before you begin to pray, you must believe that he truly wants this for you. Your faith will continue to develop more and more each time you pray and read the Word of God. For then faith comes by hearing, and hearing comes by the word of God. Now thank God in advance for adding to your life, and for giving you the desires of your heart.

Prayer

Father, I believe your Word, which tells me that I am your beloved, and you wish above all things that I prosper, and be healthy even as my soul prospers. As I continue to renew my mind, I am reminded of your will for my life. I know you want the best for me, and that it pleases you to know that I walk in the truth. In Jesus's name, amen.

Scriptures: 3 John 2 KJV; 3 John 4 KJV

NOTES

NOTES

DAY 3

Do You Know Who You Are?

You are a chosen generation, a royal priesthood, an holy nation, a peculiar people; that ye should shew forth the praises of him who hath called you out of darkness into his marvelous light. (1 Peter 2:9 KJV)

Devotion

Who are you? You are the righteousness of God in Christ Jesus. What makes you righteous? Jesus makes you righteous; it is by and through him that we have received grace. You must know who you are, because if you do not, the world will try to tell you. One of my favorite quotes is by author, motivational speaker, and prayer intercessor Cindy Trimm. She said, "In a world that demands conformity, being yourself is the hardest battle you will ever have to fight." Being yourself, being authentic, and being true - it first starts with knowing who you are. So I ask you again, who are you? First Peter 2:9 KJV says "You are a chosen generation, a royal priesthood, an holy nation, a peculiar people; that ye should shew forth the praises of him who hath called you out of darkness into his marvelous light." It begins with casting down those imaginations and pulling down strongholds, which are mindsets, from the enemy of who you are not; this way you can begin to receive revelation of who you are, from God.

Prayer

Father God, when I have a distorted view of my identity, remind me of who I am. When I feel insecure, or like I'm not enough, give me divine revelation. I realize that the weapons of my warfare are not carnal, but I know they are mighty through God and will help me to pull down those strong holds in my mind. So I will immediately begin to cast down imaginations, and every high thing that exalts itself against the knowledge of you, and I will bring into captivity every thought to the obedience of Christ. I am the head and not the tail; I am above only and not beneath. Thank you Lord, in Jesus's name, amen!

Scriptures: 2 Corinthians 10:5

NOTES

NOTES

DAY 4

See Yourself as God Sees You

And if children, then heirs; heirs of God, and joint-heirs with Christ; if so be that we suffer with him, that we may be also glorified together. (Romans 8:17 KJV)

Devotion

If you have always seen yourself in a negative light, or as someone always defeated it is time you got a new picture. For everything anyone has ever told you about yourself that does not line up with the Word of God, render it null and void. It no longer exists. Remove the defeated images out of your mind and your memory. Many people have been told very negative things in either childhood, or adulthood, about who they are. Here is the million-dollar question. How do you see yourself? As someone who is down trodden and barely making it? Or do you see yourself as more than a conqueror who is a joint-heir with Christ. Rejoice in your true and new identity. Confess who God says you are in Christ Jesus- not who the world or relatives say you are. It all starts with how you see yourself. Changing your lens, will ultimately change your life. See yourself how God sees you.

Scriptures: Romans 8:17

Prayer ▬▬▬▬▬▬▬▬▬▬▬▬▬▬▬▬▬▬▬▬▬▬▬▬▬▬

Father if you are for me, then who can be against me? Help me to get out of my mind permanently, the negative lens through which I have seen myself. When I feel miserable and unfulfilled, I will express thanksgiving and remember you are more than enough. I cancel every pessimistic, contradictory, self-defeating, and unfavorable thought right now, by casting down imaginations and every high thing that exalts itself against the knowledge of God, and bringing into captivity every thought to the obedience of Christ. As you are Jesus, so am I in this world. I will not be conformed to this world, but I shall be transformed by the renewing of my mind. In Jesus's name, amen.

Scriptures: 2 Corinthians 10:5; 1 John 4:17; Romans 12:2

NOTES

NOTES

DAY 5

Face Fear Head On

For God hath not given us the spirit of fear; but of power, and of love, and of a sound mind. (2 Timothy 1:7 KJV)

Devotion

In the book of Job, Job has a profound revelation on fear. After suffering every type of calamity a human could possibly face, Job says in 3:25 KJV, "For the thing which I greatly feared is come upon me, and that which I was afraid of is come unto me.' What we fear has the ability to come upon us. Just like when we speak in faith, and meditate on those things we do want, when we speak and constantly ruminate and meditate on things we are afraid of, they will be drawn to us. It's almost like a magnet: we attract it to us. Fear is a spirit and does not belong to you. It must be cast out. It is sent to you to abort the plans, dreams and destiny God has planned for you. Do not run from it, remember, it is an illusion to make you slow down, stop, and cower in the corner. In the next verse Job says, "I was not in safety,

17

neither had I rest, neither was I quiet; yet trouble came." The safety Job was referring to was God's protection. When we are in fear it opens up the door to the enemy. Psalm 91:1-2 NIV says, "Whoever dwells in the shelter of the Most High will rest in the shadow of the Almighty. I will say of the Lord, He is my refuge and my fortress, my God, in whom I trust." We are not to fear, but to remain stable, and fixed with our eyes on God. The devil is a lie, and you will win! Face fear head on, and get rid of it. Overcome It, with prayer, deliverance, and the Word of God.

Prayer

Heavenly Father, I thank you that you have not given me a spirit of fear, so I abolish and destroy old mindsets and procrastination; I bind and cut off the spirit of fear in the name of Jesus. For you are an amazing and all-powerful God, and fear does not reside with you; therefore it cannot reside with me. I understand that the devil comes to steal, kill, and destroy, but Jesus came that I may have life and have it more abundantly. I bind and rebuke the spirit of fear and cast it back down to the pit of hell from where it came from. Fear of the unknown, fear of my finances, fear of my future, and fear for my safety must leave me now in Jesus's name. I loose and release power, love, and a sound mind over me. I loose and release the blood of Jesus over me and over the portals of my mind. Lord Jesus, you said "Behold, I give unto you power to tread on serpents and scorpions, and over all the power of the enemy: and nothing shall by any means hurt you. "I believe it and walk in it. Thank you, Father, for you have delivered me from the power of darkness, and you have translated me into the kingdom of your dear Son. In Jesus's name. Amen.

Scriptures: Luke 10:19 KJV; John 10:10 KJV

NOTES

NOTES

DAY 6

Dream Fearlessly

And this is the confidence that we have in him, that, if we ask any thing according to his will, he heareth us: And if we know that he hear us, whatsoever we ask, we know that we have the petitions that we desired of him. (1 John 5:14 KJV)

Devotion

Many people still have dreams and desires they want to accomplish in life. Sadly, sometimes we stagnate our own growth and progress due to old mindsets, procrastination, and fears, which are almost like brick walls in our thinking. I once heard a motivational speaker say, that an acronym for fear is false evidence appearing real. But the word of God clearly tells us, "Now Faith is the substance of things hoped for, the evidence of things not seen." Scripture also clearly tells us God has not given us a spirit of fear, but of power, love, and a sound mind.

God cannot lie. If he says he will do it, he will do it. Just remember when we pray, we should ask for things that line up with the word of

God, and his will for our lives. Is it healing you desire? Is it the mate God has for you? Is it a new job, a new car, or a better place to live? All of those things line up with his will for our lives, He said in 3 John 2 KJV, "Beloved, I wish above all things that you may prosper and be in health, even as thy soul prospers." As we recall our answered prayers, and testimonies from the past, it allows your faith to increase. Stand firm in your faith, and believe and trust God.

Increase your faith by choosing to renew your mind in the word of God. Romans 10:17 KJV says, "So then faith comes by hearing, and hearing by the word of God." God will not let you down; you can trust God with your life.

Scriptures: Hebrews 11:1 KJV; 2 Timothy 1:7 KJV

Prayer

Father, I thank you that all the promises in Him are yea, and in Him Amen unto the Glory of God by us. I stand firm in faith, and I will not allow it to waver, because I know that without faith it is impossible to please the Lord. Therefore, Father I ask that if there is any unbelief in my heart, I pray that you will allow the Holy Spirit to minister to me as I read the Word of God. I want to have a complete understanding of your Word, and be steadfast and know beyond any doubt, that you are for me. I know that it pleases you to know that your children walk in the truth. I abolish and destroy old mindsets, procrastination, and fear. I walk confidently and joyfully in love, power, and a sound mind. I know that you are with me, and you are for me. You have given me your word that you will never leave me, nor forsake me. You are the lifter of my head, and you always cause me to triumph in Christ Jesus. I will forever trust you, and I know by so doing; I will go from glory to glory, and from faith to faith. In Jesus's name, amen.

Scriptures: 2 Corinthians 1:20 KJV; Psalm 3:3 KJV; 2 Corinthians 2:14 KJV

NOTES

NOTES

DAY 7

Dream Big

And from the days of John the Baptist until now the kingdom of heaven suffereth violence, and the violent take it by force. (Matthew 11:12 KJV)

Devotion

Along with the name of Jesus, the Word of God, and the Blood of Jesus, Prayer is a mighty weapon. It can achieve the same results and even greater results as any man made weapon here on earth. Hebrews 4:12 KJV tells us that "the word of God is quick, powerful, and sharper than any two edged sword, piercing even to the dividing asunder of soul and spirit, and of the joints and marrow, and is a discerner of the thoughts and intents of the heart." With prayer we are attacking the spirit realm. The word of God tells us that since the days of John the Baptist, until now the kingdom of heaven suffereth violence, and the violent take it by force. Be relentless in your prayers, and never give up.

Scriptures: Matthew 11:12 KJV

Prayer

Father God, You direct my path, and order my steps. Nothing can stop, block, or hinder what you have for me any longer. If God be for me, who can be against me? What you have for me is for me, and I command it to come to me in abundance. I receive it now in Jesus's name, amen.

Scriptures: Proverbs 3:6 KJV

NOTES

NOTES

DAY 8

Write It Down

And the Lord answered me, and said, write the vision, and make it plain upon tables, that he may run that readeth it. For the vision is yet for an appointed time, but at the end it shall speak, and not lie: though it tarry, wait for it; because it will surely come, it will not tarry. (Habakkuk 2:2-3 KJV)

Devotion

Write down what you want for your life. What is it that you aspire to do? Where do you want to go? What do you want? It's very important that you write it down, because once it's before you, you have more clarity. You'll see it daily, and begin to speak it. Keep it before you, and ultimately you will have what you say! I ask you again, what do you see for yourself, and where do you see yourself going? Write the vision.

Scripture: Habakkuk 2:2 KJV; Mark 11:23 KJV Scriptures: Habakkuk 2:2 KJV; Mark 11:23 KJV

Prayer

Father God, I stand on your word that says you shall give me the desires of my heart if I also delight myself in you! Help me to focus on you, and find great pleasure and joy in you while doing so. I know you have a plan for my life, and I will see it happen. As I write the vision, I will run with it, and not become weary while waiting. I know and believe that though it may take a moment to come, it will surely come to pass, and it will NOT fail. In Jesus's name, amen.

Scriptures: Psalm 37:4 KJV

NOTES

NOTES

DAY 9

Your Gift Opens
Doors For You

A mans gift maketh room for him, and bringeth him before great
men. (Proverbs 18:16 KJV)

Devotion

What is your gift? A gift is described as a natural ability or talent.
Many people say they have no idea what their purpose or what their
gift is. However, I believe many people do know what their purpose or
gift is, but are reluctant to move in that area of their lives. Once you
obtain clarity, vision and revelation concerning the gift and talents
God has placed in you, you can walk in it with total confidence. Your
gift creates opportunities and spaces for your gift to influence and bless
others. Your gift is what you will be known for, it should identify you.
Do what you were born to do, not what your family or friends tell you
is going to make you money.

Be a leader, be set apart, soar like an eagle, and trust the process. Your gift will help you to reach your destiny and complete the vision. When you desire to share your gift with the world, and give your gift back to God, the floodgates of Heaven and doors will open with an abundance of opportunities to bring your gift before others. The word of God tells us that "Every good gift and and every perfect gift is from above, and cometh down from the Father of lights, with whom is no variableness, neither shadow of turning." That same scripture in the Message version says, "The gifts are rivers of light cascading down from the Father of Light." Be careful and wise how you use your gifts. Remember they are not for us, but for those we will reach, and bless, and ultimately for God to get the glory. You are giving your gift back to God when you use it the way He designed it to be used. It would be selfish of us to think for one minute, all the gifts we have, are for our own use and our pleasure alone.

Scriptures: James 1:17 KJV, and MSG

Prayer

Father, I thank you that the gifts you have placed in me shall begin to create amazing opportunities for me to bless others. I will not sit on my gifts but I will use them for the good of your kingdom, for you to get the glory. Please continue to make my gifts known to me, so that I may walk in them with total confidence. I am forever humbled by your love for me, and how you have entrusted me with these gifts. I decree and declare, that my gift shall make room for me, and bring me before great men. Doors shall open that no man can shut. I thank you that, you who have begun a good work in me shall complete it until the day of Jesus Christ. In Jesus's name, amen.

Scriptures: Job 22:28 KJV

NOTES

NOTES

DAY 10

Who Told You, You Couldn't Do That?

I can do all things through Christ which strengthen me. (Philippians 4:13 KJV)

Devotion

Stop sharing your big dreams with small minded people...you are wasting your time. Be careful who you share your dreams with. Everyone does not always have your best interest in mind, and it actually has nothing to do with you. It's really about their defeatist attitude. Usually people who tell you, you can't do that, it's because they didn't, and no one else around them did either. In their eyes they never achieved what they wanted. Forgive them, but run from people like that. They may say they're protecting you, but they are not. I once heard respected author, prayer warrior, and motivational speaker Cindy Trimm say, "silence the naysayers, these people are called abortionists." Life and death are in the power of the tongue, so you want people around you who will tell you "Yes you can, you will get there," and not the opposite. You want people who are in agreement with you, not opposing you. They may say, you don't have the right look, the right experience, or know the right people, but may I remind you, that if you are in Christ, all things are possible with Him. He always causes you to triumph, and He is no respecter of persons. If God be for you, who can be against you. Now that's good news!

Scripture: Proverbs 18:21 KJV

Prayer

Father, I thank you that you are No respecter of persons, what you'll do for one, you'll do for another and that includes me. Please place around me people who have my best interest at heart. Reveal to me, those who are opposing me, speaking against me, or are using me. I forgive them from the bottom of my heart, and I ask you that you help them to have a deeper revelation of who you are, and how whatever we want in life that is in your will, is completely obtainable. I know that with you, all things are possible, and I can do and achieve all things through Christ who strengthens me. I cancel every negative word that has been spoken against me or my destiny, and I loose divine success and prosperity. My hope and trust is completely in you, and because of that, my strength shall be renewed. I shall mount up with wings like eagles; I will run, and not be weary; I shall walk and not faint. In Jesus's name, amen.

Scriptures: Isaiah 40:31 KJV

NOTES

NOTES

DAY 11

Who Told You, You Are Too Old?

He staggered not at the promise of God through unbelief; but was strong in faith, giving glory to God; (Romans 4:20 KJV)

Devotion

You are never too old. Throughout the Bible God used people of all ages to accomplish the unimaginable, and blessed and gave favor to those who thought their time had come and gone. Take Abraham for example. God told Abram that he would be a father...at nearly 100 years old. His wife Sara was also well past childbearing age. God changed his name from Abram to Abraham; which means father of many nations. The Bible says Abraham BELIEVED God, and it was counted unto him for righteousness. Is there anything too hard for God? The answer is No. The bible says...Abraham staggered not at the promises of God through unbelief; but was strong in faith, giving glory to God. Never, ever, allow your chronological age to stop you from fulfilling your destiny. See yourself as God sees you...able to do all things through Christ.

Scriptures: Romans 4:3 KJV; Romans 4:20-21 KJV; Phillipians 4:13 KJV

Prayer ══

Father I thank you for restoring the years to me. Years that the cankerworm and the palm have eaten up. You are a God of restoration, and refreshing, and my youth is renewed like the eagles. Regardless of my age, I decree and declare this is my time, and my season. I thank you that I can decree a thing, and it shall be established. According to Revelation 3: 8 you have opened doors no man can shut. For nothing shall be impossible for me with you. Your word says that as I age, it is a Blessing from you. I will no longer allow my age to be a hindrance for me pursuing the things I have always wanted to do. You said you will give me the desires of my heart, if I delight myself in you. I thank you for it in advance, in Jesus's name, amen.

Scriptures: Revelation 3:8 KJV ; Joel 2:25 KJV; Psalm 103:5 KJV

NOTES

NOTES

DAY 12

It's Never Too Late

Seek first the kingdom of God and his righteousness; and all these things shall be added to you. (Matthew 6:33 KJV)

Devotion

I assure you, God has not forgotten about you. He still hears, and answers our prayers. Maybe you want to write a book, go back to school, or even start an entirely new career like I did. Whatever it is, be clear, concise, and remain focused. Maybe your desire is to be married, or have a child. Its. Never. Too. Late.

Whatever it is, do not be anxious for it. Anxiety will become a distraction, and will not allow you to be at peace, so you can hear God. Instead, with prayer, petition, supplication, and thanksgiving, make your request known to God, and the peace of God, while your waiting, shall guard your heart, and your mind in Christ Jesus. It's never too late.

Scriptures: Philippians 4:6-7 KJV

Prayer

Heavenly Father, I thank you that you have restored the years that have been stolen from me. You have awakened in me once again the desires of my heart. I shall run the race which has been set before me. I understand the race is not given to the swift but to the one that endures to the end. I thought it was too late for me, but I am reminded that as I wait upon You, You shall renew my strength. I shall mount up with wings like eagles; I shall run, and not be weary; and I shall walk, and not faint. For you have redeemed the time. In Jesus's name, amen.

Scriptures: Ecclesiastes 9:11 KJV; Matthew 24:13 KJV; Isaiah 40:31 KJV

NOTES

NOTES

DAY 13

Who Told You, You Are Too Young?

I am young in years, and you are old; that is why I was fearful, not daring to tell you what I know. I thought age should speak, advanced years should teach wisdom. But it is the spirit in a person, the breath of the Almighty that gives them understanding. It is not only the old who are wise, not only the aged who understand what is right. Therefore I say: listen to me; I too will tell you what I know. (Job 32:6-10 NIV)

Devotion

You are never too young. If God gave you the idea, the thought or the desire, or gave you the inspiration to do something, He will use you as a vessel to see to it that it happens. Never second guess yourself because of your youthful age, and never, ever allow people to intimidate you because of your young age. God told the Prophet

Jeremiah to go out and do what He told him to do. The Lord told him, "Do not say, 'I am too young. You must go to everyone I send you to and say whatever I command you. Do not be afraid of them, for I am with you and will rescue you," declares the Lord. Let that also be an order for you. God can use anyone regardless of their age. Age really is just a number.

Scriptures: Jeremiah 1:7-8 NIV

Prayer

Father I rejoice right now that though I may be young in age, I am more than able to do the things you have assigned me to do. Just as you gave the Prophet Jeremiah an assignment you have given me one too. I will no longer be reluctant to carry it out, because I know that you are with me. My age is not a hindrance, but an advantage; for the Word also tells me according to Proverbs 20:29 that "the glory of the young is their strength." I receive it in Jesus's name, amen.

Scriptures: Proverbs 20:29 NLT; 1 Peter 5:7 KJV

NOTES

NOTES

God Is For You

What shall we then say to these things? If God be for us, who can be against us? (Romans 8:31 KJV)

Devotion

Never Give Up. Never ever give up. Do you know your Heavenly Father wants to bless you? His Favor has been released and activated in your life. He has given you permission to dream. Just ask for what you want. All the promises in Him are yea, and Amen. He is an Intentional God. He is able to do exceeding and abundantly above all that we could ask or think. Take pleasure in that.

Scriptures: 2 Corinthians 1:20 KJV; Ephesians 3:20 KJV

Prayer

Thank you Father, that I will succeed in whatever I choose to do, and light will shine on the road ahead of me. I thank you that if You be for me, who can be against me. You are an Intentional God, with a great plan for my life. Now, Thanks be unto you, that even when I am at my lowest, and what feels like my darkest hour, You always cause me to triumph in Christ Jesus, In Jesus' name, amen.

Scriptures: 2 Corinthians 2:14 KJV

NOTES

NOTES

DAY 15

Desire Wisdom

Wisdom is the principal thing; therefore get wisdom: and with all thy getting get understanding. (Proverbs 4:7 KJV)

Devotion

The fear of the Lord is the beginning of wisdom, but fools despise wisdom and instruction. Honoring God in your life and keeping His word is vital. Ask yourself... Am I honoring God through my actions and my words, when I am placed in situations where I am tested to react and behave in ways that do not bring him glory? Could this be holding me back? If you are not sure just ask him. He will give you the wisdom you need to go forward in life, and to make sound decisions. When you receive the wisdom you need, make sure you get an understanding. You need a discerning and a revelation that will propel you at lightning speed to move forward.

Scriptures: Proverbs 1:7 DRB; Proverbs 4:7 KJV

Prayer

Father I need wisdom. I need wisdom to help me to understand areas in my life that need improvement. Your word tells me I can ask for wisdom and you will give it to me. In every area of my life I want to prosper. If I am standing in my own way please tell me, and help me to discern and understand the instructions you give me; and give me the tenacity and strength to do it. I thank you that I have received the spirit of wisdom and revelation, in the knowledge of Jesus, which continues to enlighten the eyes of my understanding. In Jesus's name, amen.

Scriptures: Ephesians 1:17-18

NOTES

NOTES

DAY 16

Check Your Heart

Therefore I say unto you, What things soever ye desire, when ye pray, believe that ye receive them, and ye shall have them. And when ye stand praying, forgive, if ye have ought against any: that your Father also which is in heaven may forgive you your trespasses. (Mark 11:24-25 KJV)

Devotion

Ask yourself these questions. What is your daily walk like? Are you walking in love? If not, you should; your success depends on it. Just as we perfect our faith walk, we also have to perfect our love walk. It is imperative, and an order from God. We are commanded to love one another. A command is an authoritative order instructing, ordering and requiring us to do something. In this case it is a direct order from God telling us to love, not as we love, but with the love of God. We've all been hurt and disappointed, but please, let it go, it's not worth it. Forgive those who have wronged you, and resist the urge to retaliate, or speak harshly against them. Bless them instead. By so doing, you unknowingly create more opportunities in your life for God to bless you.

Scriptures: John 13:34 KJV; Luke 6:28 NLT,KJV

Prayer

Father God, create in me a clean heart; and renew a right spirit within me. I repent for holding hostile or unforgiving feelings in my heart, against those who have wronged me, and I ask you to forgive me. I thank you for all the times you have forgiven me, and wish to extend the same grace and mercy to (name the person(s). I now forgive (name the person or persons) for everything (or name the hurts). I no longer hold on to any bitterness, anguish, disappointment, or pain any longer. As long as I hold on to it, you cannot do anything with it. Your word tells me to cast ALL of my cares and burdens on you, because you care for me. I now release it, let it go, give it to you, and move on with the life you have given me. I also release the blessing of the Lord on (name the person(s) and anyone else who has hurt me. I ask that you would increase them, more and more, and that they would grow in you. I pray that the love of God will overtake them, because you love and care for them, just like you do for me. Thank you Jesus, for setting me free! In Jesus's name, amen.

Scriptures: Psalm 51:10 KJV

NOTES

NOTES

DAY 17

While You Are Waiting Help Others

And I sought for a man among them that should make up the hedge, and stand in the gap before me for the land, that I should not destroy it: but I found none. (Ezekiel 22:30 KJV)

Devotion

Get yourself off your mind, by helping others to accomplish their dreams. It actually helps you also. Praying for others in their time of need is our duty. The Lord said to the Prophet Ezekiel, that he looked for someone to stand in the gap, to intercede, to pray for the land but He found no one. Sometimes we can be so focused on our own needs that we fail to pray and be concerned about others. We should have compassion for others and be ready to pray for their needs as well. Have you ever been awakened in the middle of the night and someone was on your mind? Or maybe you randomly thought about someone totally out of the blue. When that happens we should be in prayer for them. When we pray for others, we're also blessed. We are our brother's keeper.

Scriptures: 1 Thessalonians 5:17 KJV

Prayer

Father God, thank you for showing me the need to pray for others. There are things that I desire but I also want to see your will come to pass in other people's lives as well. Your word tells me to comfort, strengthen and to encourage one another. I am strong in the Lord and in the power of His might and I pray in the interest of others (or name person) as they pursue success. Show me who I can pray for and encourage today, In Jesus's name, amen.

Scriptures: 1 Thessalonians 5:11 ESV; Hebrews 10:23-25 ESV; Ephesians 6:10 KJV

NOTES

NOTES

DAY 18

Don't Give Up

For the Lord God will help me; therefore shall I not be confounded: therefore have I set my face like a flint, and I know that I shall not be ashamed. (Isaiah 50:7 KJV)

Devotion

Keep your face set like a flint. Flint is a very hard, sedimentary, crystallized rock. That scripture represents being strong-willed, determined, and relentless in the midst of whatever we are going through. Come what may, being bold, courageous, and valiant in adversity, in order to accomplish what God told you and has called you to do. The only fight we are to have as believers is the good fight of faith. Waiting for God to show up is really not long if we learn to wait in faith. With faith there is no time. Faith overrides time. Faith based prayer, speaking the word of God, and calling things that be not as though they were; because they already are in the spirit realm.

You're just waiting for them to manifest naturally. Using your mouth you can change your life through the word of God. Starting right now.

Scriptures: 1 Timothy 6:12 KJV; Romans 4:17 KJV; Isaiah 50:7 NLT

Prayer

Thank you Father, that I am encouraged through your word, which I know to be absolutely true. In the midst of whatever I endure I can go on with strength and tenacity. I believe because you help me, I will not be disgraced. Therefore I have set my face like flint, and I know I will not be put to shame. For you are the lifter of my head, and you always cause me to triumph in Christ Jesus. The will you have for my life shall come to pass, In Jesus's name, amen.

Scriptures: Psalm 3:3 KJV; 2 Corinthians 2:14 KJV

NOTES

NOTES

DAY 19

Stop Looking Back

Brethren, I count not myself to have apprehended: but this one thing I do, forgetting those things which are behind, and reaching forth unto those things which are before, (Philippians 3:13 KJV)

Devotion

Stop chasing what is not yours. Stop going back to doors that have been closed, and locked. God has a very specific plan for your life; that includes your career, people, places, and assignments. Philippians 3:13 in the Message Translation makes it very plain. "I'm not saying that I have this all together, that I have it made. But I am well on my way, reaching out for Christ, who has so wondrously reached out for me. Friends, don't get me wrong: By no means do I count myself an expert in all of this, but I've got my eye on the goal, where God is beckoning us onward—to Jesus. I'm off and running and I'm not turning back." MSG

Stay focused on your goal, and move forward. Trust God. Turning, going, or looking back signifies an uncertainty about your future, and is an indication your faith may need an upgrade. Most of us are guilty of this at least once in our lives, but there is never a reason to go back or look back in any situation; especially since God has promised you a hope, and a future. All it does is impede your progress in reaching and fulfilling your destiny.

Scriptures: Jeremiah 29:11 KJV

Prayer

Heavenly Father, thank you for revelation on how looking back hinders my progress in life, and my walk with you. I have looked back for the last time. I now forget the former things and dwell no more on the past, for you are truly doing a new thing, and now it springs up. Even though I have experienced and endured much in my life, I can truly say I am an overcomer by the Blood of the Lamb, and by the word of my testimony. So finally, I am forgetting those things, which are behind, and reaching forth unto those things, which are before, and press toward the mark for the prize of the high calling of God in Christ. In Jesus's name, amen.

Scriptures: Revelation 12:11 KJV; Philippians 3:13-14 KJV

NOTES

NOTES

DAY 20

Beware Of The Dream Killers

I am far from oppression, and fear does not come near me. You shall be far from oppression, for you shall not fear; and from terror, for it shall not come near you. (Isaiah 54:14 ESV)

Devotion

There will always be naysayers. There will always be those people who will give you their reasons for why they believe your dream is unattainable. Stop sharing your big dreams with small-minded people... your wasting your time. If God be for you, who can be against you.

I say to you, DON'T LISTEN TO THEM. TUNE THEM OUT. Sometimes people are not even aware they are being used by the enemy to stop, or slow down your progress. If God placed that desire in your heart, it is achievable. With man, some things are possible, but with God, all things are possible.

Scriptures: Matthew 19:26 NIV

Prayer

Father, I thank you that if you be for me, who can be against me. According to Jeremiah 29:11 NIV, you have plans to "prosper me, and not to harm me, plans to give me hope and a future." I fear no man, and the blessing of the Lord rests upon me. I have favor with you and favor with man. I receive the overwhelming love you have for me, and I say thank you that your will is for me to prosper. You have opened doors that no man can shut, and I walk right through them. I can do all things through Christ, which strengthens me, because I am more than a conqueror. In Jesus's name, Amen.

Scriptures: Romans 8:31 KJV

NOTES

NOTES

DAY 21

Who Do You Believe?

What shall we then say to these things? If God be for us, who can be against us? (Romans 8:31 KJV)

Devotion

Ask yourself these questions. Who is speaking in to your life? Where are they now? Where are they going? Where have they been? Be mindful of who you are allowing to speak into your life, and give you advice. God's word is infallible. If He said you are the head, and not the tail, above only, and not beneath, then that is what you are. When people show you who they are, believe them; the first time. Yes it's nice to have the support and encouragement of others but do not allow it to hold you back if you don't get it. Majority of the time when people are not supportive it is because they never had support. You've heard the saying, "hurt people hurt others." Well, oppressed and defeated people; oppress others. What should you say in response to the naysayers? If God be for me, who can be against me? Believe God. He can't lie. If God said it, believe it, and that should settle it.

Scriptures: Romans 8:31 NIV; Numbers 23:19 KJV; Titus 1:2 NIV; Hebrews 6:18 KJV

Prayer

Father, In the name of Jesus, I decree and declare I'm more than a conqueror. I can do what you say I can do, and I have what you say I have. I'm a joint-heir with Christ, therefore I have what Jesus has. Let God be true and every man a liar. I believe with all my heart that God is for me, and if He is for me, the who, is irrelevant. Thank you God that you are always in my corner. In Jesus's name, amen.

Scriptures: Romans 3:4 NIV, 8:17 KJV

NOTES

NOTES

DAY 22

What Do You Believe?

Let God be true and every man a liar. (Romans 3:4 KJV)

Devotion

Do you believe that with God, all things are possible, or does it just sound nice to say? Your destiny rests in the hands of your faith. To reach your destiny you must have faith. No one can stop you but you. No enemy, no neighbor, no co-worker, no family member, no ex, no one. No one can stop you, but you. In the words of Visionary leader, and pastor, Dr. Bill Winston, "Your future is in your heart." You must understand that being a believer is a lifestyle. Not just something you do on Sunday morning. The word of God is infallible. If the word of God says you can do all things through Christ which strengthens you, then it is undoubtedly true.

Scriptures: Philippians 4:13 KJV; Matthew 19:26 NIV

Prayer

Father, Your word says that it pleases you to know that your children walk in the truth. Today is a new day, and a new opportunity for me to draw closer to you. When you say I'm more than a conqueror, I believe it, when you say nothing is impossible with you, I believe it. When you say I can do all things through Christ who strengthens me, I believe it. Let God be true, and every man a liar. If my faith needs to be strengthened, please increase it. According to Romans 12:3 KJV; you have given to every man the measure of faith. I know that without faith it is impossible to please you. So right now, in the midst of what looks impossible, I lean not to my own understanding, but in all of my ways I shall acknowledge You, and you will direct my paths. Glory to God, In Jesus's name, amen.

Scriptures: Romans 8:37 KJV; Luke 1:37 KJV; Philippians 4:13 KJV; Romans 3:4 KJV

NOTES

NOTES

DAY 23

What Do You See?

Then Elisha prayed and said, "O LORD, I pray, open his eyes that he may see" And the LORD opened the servant's eyes and he saw; and behold, the mountain was full of horses and chariots of fire all around Elisha. (2 Kings 6:17 NIV)

Devotion

The word Rhema means the spoken or revealed word of God, which is revealed by the Holy Spirit and spiritually understood. Rhema brings light and revelation. The prophet Elisha prayed unto the Lord for his servant's eyes to be open, for him to SEE that even though a large number of horses and chariots had surrounded the city, there was no reason for him to fear. Elisha told his servant to fear not, for there were more with them, than against them; but Elisha needed him to SEE it for himself. Which is why he prayed for his spiritual eyes to be opened.

Having Rhema Faith is vital for manifesting your prayer in the natural. It's imperative that we see with our spiritual eyes. You are not looking at what you see happening in the natural, but what has already been established before the foundation of the world. Begin to see your promise come to pass. See your dream come to pass. See yourself reaching your destiny. If you are having a difficult time seeing your dream come to fruition, how about starting with looking unto Jesus and Fixing your eyes on Him, who is the author and finisher of your faith.

Scriptures: Hebrews 12:2 KJV

Prayer

Father God, as I begin to see your promises for my life come to pass, I ask that you would have me to begin to see on a deeper spiritual level. I ask that you, the father of Glory would give unto me the spirit of wisdom and revelation in the knowledge of him: and that the eyes of my understanding would be enlightened; that I may know what the hope of his calling is, and what the riches of the glory of his inheritance in the saints. I pray that just like you opened the servant's eyes, you would also open my eyes. That I may see in greater spiritual depth the Excellency of your power, but also that I may see myself already walking in the promises you have stored up for me. In Jesus's name, amen.

Scriptures: Ephesians 1:17-18 KJV

NOTES

NOTES

DAY 24

Make Sure You Are Not The One Stopping You

I can do all things through Christ who strengthens me. (Philippians 4:13 NKJV)

Devotion

Who told you, you couldn't do that? Make sure it's not you. Motivational speaker Les Brown, tells a story in one of his motivational speeches about two little boys playing out on a frozen lake or pond during the winter. As they got further out one of the boys fell through the ice. The little boy that was still on top of the ice tried desperately to save his friend; he could see him but he couldn't reach him. He looked around and saw a tree and broke off a branch, ran back to where his friend was, and began to beat the ice, broke it, and miraculously saved his friend. When the paramedics showed up they were able to revive the little boy. They couldn't understand how this small boy was able to save his friend. An older gentleman who was there told the paramedics, "I can tell you how he did it. There was no one there to tell him that he couldn't do it." The little boy never told himself he couldn't do it either. He knew he could. This is essential. The only person who can stop you is you. Do not let yourself stand in the way of your success, or your blessings.

Prayer

Father you have made me fearfully and wonderfully made, therefore I do not doubt what I can or cannot do. I rejoice in my identity in Jesus. I am complete in Him, Who is the Head of all principality and power, and I have the Greater One living in me; because greater is He Who is in me than he who is in the world. With God all things are possible, and I am well equipped and have the mind of Christ which enables me to do it. In Jesus's name, amen.

Scriptures: Psalm 139:14 KJV; Jeremiah 31:3 KJV; John 1:16 GNT; Colossians 2:10 KJV; 1 John 4:4 KJV; 1 Corinthians 2:16 KJV

NOTES

NOTES

Your Miracle, Is In Your Mouth

Calleth those things that be not, as though they were. (Romans 4:17 KJV)

Devotion

Returning to school and starting off in the field of Television Broadcast News after the age of 30 was very challenging, but with God, I persevered. Even though I had already earned a degree, and had a rewarding career in Healthcare and Social Services for many years, I always wanted to be a Broadcast Journalist. As a child, I used to watch female broadcasters and tell my parents "That's what I want to do! I'm a good writer, I can do that."

As I got older, MANY people told me how impossible this dream of mine was, but I would not receive those comments. I believed in my heart, with God all things were possible. I realized my miracle was in my mouth, I began to speak and call what I wanted to come forth. I was calling myself a Journalist, a News Reporter, and an Anchor before I stepped foot into my first job. One day I just showed up at one particular station, and I knew that job was mine. I claimed the position as my own, and claimed the station as the first station that would give me my start. I held my head high in confidence, and said to myself "If God be for me, who can be against me." I felt the very presence of God with me during my interview, and I knew beyond a shadow of a doubt, I was walking in the favor of God. To God be the Glory, I was hired two weeks later, and my dream manifested in the natural. God will open doors that NO man can shut.

Scriptures: Revelation 3:8 NIV; Romans 8:31 KJV

Prayer

Father God, I am truly excited about my future. You alone, are my door opener. Revelations 3:8 says "you have set before me an open door, and NO man can shut it: for you know I have little strength, YET I have kept your word and have NOT denied your name." I can call things that be not, as though they were, until they are. Glory to God. I take that authoritative position now, and decree and declare (name what you want, that's in God's will), and no good thing shall be kept from me. I know that some things are possible with man, but ALL things are possible with you. For you my God, have loved me with an everlasting love. I thank you Lord, that from the fullness of your grace, I have received one blessing after another. I will always be forever mindful to give you the praise, the honor and the Glory you deserve. In Jesus name, Amen.

Scriptures: Revelations 3:8 NIV; Jeremiah 31:3 KJV; John 1:16 GNT

NOTES

NOTES

DAY 26

Stay Full Of Joy

For this day is holy unto our Lord: neither be ye sorry; for the joy of the Lord is your strength. (Nehemiah 8:10 KJV)

Devotion

Regardless of how long you have been waiting remain joyful in the Lord. It is your strength. You cannot allow defeated thoughts to remain in your mind. It all starts with a thought, and it is a trick of the enemy. If you're joy is zapped, where is your strength? Yes, fight the good fight of faith, but remember the joy of the Lord is your strength. It is God's desire that we are full of joy, despite what's going on around us. Happiness is not the same as joy; happiness is temporary, and requires things are right in every area of your life. Joy comes from within, and is not dependent upon external circumstances. John 15:11 ESV says, "These things I have spoken to you, that my joy may be in you, and that your joy may be full."

Scriptures: Romans 15:13 NIV; John 15:11 KJV; Nehemiah 8:10 KJV

Prayer

Thank you Father, that the Joy of the Lord is my strength, and you have made known to me the path of life. In your presence there is fullness of joy; and at your right hand are pleasures forevermore. God, even on my worse day I will not allow the things of the world to take my joy from me. This joy I have the world didn't give it, and the world can't take it away. Father your word says let all those that put their trust in You rejoice: let them ever shout for joy, because you defend and protect them: let those who also love your name be joyful in you. In Jesus's name, amen.

Scriptures: Psalm 5:11 NKJV; Psalm 16:11 NKJV

NOTES

NOTES

DAY 27

We Are The Ones, The World Is Waiting For

Trust in the Lord with all thine heart; and lean not unto thine understanding. In all thy ways acknowledge him, and he shall direct thy paths. (Proverbs 3:5-6 KJV)

Devotion

Even though we desire what we want, the Spirit of God must lead us. The world is waiting for righteous, just, bold, honest people with integrity to come forth. You have something to say, you have something to do, but I caution you. Do not do it without God. When we do things without His guidance, direction, and approval, we are setting ourselves up for failure. There are people counting on you who you have not even met yet, and many of them you never will. However, they are waiting on you to execute, demonstrate, and be fearless in what you have already been predestined to do. Do not blow it, by leaning on your own understanding. For as many as are led by the spirit of God, they are the Sons of God. Trust in the Lord with all thine heart; and lean not unto thine understanding. In all thy ways acknowledge him, and he shall direct thy paths.

Scriptures: Proverbs 3:5-6 KJV; Romans 8: 14 KJV; Psalm 143:10 NIV

Prayer

Father, I commit my ways unto you and as I go forth into the things for which you have called me, I have full confidence that you have equipped me. I will listen for You. I shall not waste time in the muck and the mire...toiling, getting nowhere, and trying to figure out things on my own. Help me to keep my focus on you. Distractions will come, but do not let them consume me. Help me to crucify my flesh, and be led by, and walk in the spirit. There are people waiting on me, people counting on me. I will not let them or you down. Help me NOT to lean to my own understanding, but in all my ways acknowledge you, and you shall direct my paths. In Jesus's name, amen.

Scriptures: Proverbs 3:5-6 KJV; Galatians 2:20 KJV

NOTES

NOTES

DAY 28

Being Spirit Led

For all who are being led by the Spirit of God, these are sons of God. (Romans 8:14 NASB)

Devotion

Being Spirit led is crucial as you go through life. Listening to and for God is vital as you get closer to where God is taking you. While you are waiting for doors to open; doing what God tells you to do, gets you there much quicker. You must come out of your flesh. You have to operate on a different level. A higher level. You need to know when to act and not just react.

It is important to know when you are operating in jealousy, envy, unforgiveness, strife, hatred and other way's that may be causing you to behave out of your flesh. How do you treat people? The word tells us that the fruits of the spirit are love, joy, peace, patience, kindness, goodness, faithfulness, gentleness, and self-control. Even if your faith is high, and you are strong in prayer, but you are not walking in love, it keeps what you are believing God for suspended. In 1 Corinthians 13:2-8, the Apostle Paul talks about though you may be prophetic, a giver to the poor and have high faith that can move mountains, all of that is virtually null and void if you have no love. Please remember this, because it is vital for your growth in God and for your prayers to be answered.

The quicker you are led by God, the sooner you will see your desires manifest in the natural. Practice walking in the spirit. When God tells you to call someone, do it. When He tells you to keep quiet when you want to give someone a piece of your mind, do it. And When He tells you to go left, do it, you very well may be avoiding a disaster on the right. In all things, be Spirit led.

Scriptures: Galatians 5:22-23 NLT, Corinthians 13:2-8 KJV

Prayer

Lord God, I understand to be carnal minded, thinking and operating in my flesh is death, but to be spiritually minded, walking in the spirit and being led by the spirit of God is life and peace. Father, teach me to do Your will. You are my God; let your spirit lead me on level ground. Unstop my ears so I may hear you perfectly clear. Align my hearing and my seeing with your word and your will. Your word says, For they that are led by the Spirit of God, they are the Sons of God. I receive that now, In Jesus's name, amen.

Scriptures: Romans 8:5-6 KJV; Romans 8:14 KJV; Psalm 143:10 NIV

NOTES

NOTES

DAY 29

Trust God With
All Your Heart

But my God shall supply all your need according to his riches in glory by Christ Jesus. (Phillipians 4:19 KJV)

Devotion

Do you believe God, or do you just believe in God? There is a difference. Scripture says in the book of James, that even the demons believe in God, and they tremble; but do they believe God? Of course not. One of the biggest ways we show the Lord we trust and believe him is through our actions. How are your actions communicating to God that not only do you have faith, but you also believe and trust him? Abraham believed God so much that he offered his son Isaac on the altar. His faith and his actions were on one accord.

The bible says his faith was made complete and perfect by what he did. Yes, you can have perfect faith. Now that is trusting God with ALL of your heart.

Scriptures: James 2:21-22 NIV, James 2:21-22 GNT; Proverbs 3:5 KJV; James 2:19 KJV

Prayer

I have no lack, for I know that everything I need is already taken care of. I trust you with everything. I believe your word, which tells me to trust you with all of my heart, and lean not to my own understanding, but in all of my ways I will acknowledge you, and you shall make my path straight.

Thank you for supplying everything I need according to your riches in glory by Christ Jesus. Let my life be a witness to you through my actions that not only do I believe in you, but I also believe you. In Jesus's name, amen.

Scriptures: Proverbs 3:5-6 KJV; Philippians 4:19 KJV

NOTES

NOTES

DAY 30

Keep Calm...God Is Working

Do not be anxious about anything, but in every situation, by prayer and petition, with thanksgiving, present your requests to God. And the peace of God, which transcends all understanding, will guard your hearts and your minds in Christ Jesus. (Philippians 4:6-7 NIV)

Devotion

Be Anxious for NOTHING. When we are anxious, we are not in faith. Anxiety vexes or frustrates your spirit, which causes your mind to ruminate on negative thoughts such as, "what if it doesn't work?" or "what if I don't make it?" However, I ask you, "What if it does work," and, "What happens when you do make it?" The word of God tells us to be anxious for nothing. Decree you have the peace of God that passes all understanding regarding every concern in your life. After all, you can decree a thing, and it shall be established.

Scriptures: Philippians 4:6-7 NIV; Job 22:28 KJV

Prayer

Father, I will be anxious for nothing. I have presented my request to you, and now the peace of God, which transcends all understanding shall guard my heart and my mind in Christ Jesus. You are the lifter of my head, and you have made me triumphant in Christ Jesus. I have the mind of Christ Jesus and I will only think on thoughts that are pure, honest, just, praise worthy, and lovely. If there is ANY virtue, and if there is ANY praise, I will think on these things. In Jesus's name, amen.

Scriptures: Psalm 3:3 ESV; 2 Corinthians 2:14-16 KJV; Philippians 4:8 KJV

NOTES

NOTES

DAY 31

Rest In God

There remaineth therefore a rest to the people of God. For he that is entered into his rest, he also hath ceased from his own works, as God did from his. Let us labour therefore to enter into that rest, lest any man fall after the same example of unbelief. (Hebrews 4:9-11 KJV)

Devotion

Be at Peace, and Be at Rest. If you are doing the work, God rests; if you rest, God works. Your job is to trust and believe. He will keep those in perfect peace who keep their mind stayed on Him. Allow the peace of God to rest upon you, and remember He is with you, and for you. You are either going to believe that all the promises of God in him are yea, and in him, Amen, or you are not. That same scripture in another translation reads, "For no matter how many promises God has made, they are "Yes" in Christ. And so through him the "Amen" is spoken by us to the glory of God." The choice is yours. Choose well.

I decree your breakthrough will happen suddenly and unexpectedly. Be ready for it.

May this blessing keep you forever mindful that all things are possible with God. Now unto Him who is able to (carry out his purpose and) do superabundantly more than all that we dare ask or think (infinitely beyond our greatest prayers, hopes, or dreams), according to His power that is at work within us, in Jesus's name, Amen.

Scriptures: Amos 9:13 MSG; Ephesians 3:20 AMP; 2 Corinthians 1:20 KJV, and NIV

Prayer

Heavenly Father, I am excited and ready for my breakthrough! I will rest in you because I am firmly rooted, built up, established in my faith and overflowing with gratitude. I have put off the old man and have put on the new man, which is renewed in knowledge, after the image of him, Who created him. It is a finished work. As I rest in you, I believe your word, which says, this is the confidence we have in approaching you: that if we ask anything according to your will, you hear us, and if we know that you hear us, whatever we ask, we know that we have what we asked of you. Now thanks be unto God, which always causes me to triumph in Christ Jesus! In Jesus's name, amen.

Scriptures: 1 John 5:14-15 NIV; 2 Corinthians 2:14 KJV; Colossians 3:10 KJV

PRAYER TO START
A NEW LIFE
(PRAYER OF SALVATION)

If you are unsaved, or desire a deeper relationship with the Lord, I encourage you to do it immediately. God loves you so much, and only wants the best for your life. Regardless of what you have come from, or gone through, He desires a relationship with you. He said in His word, I have loved you with an everlasting love (Jeremiah 31:3 NIV) If God has touched your heart, and you know it's time for you to take that next step, please pray this prayer.

Father God I come to you in the name of your son Jesus Christ. According to 1 John 3:8 KJV, he that commits sin is of the devil; for the devil sins from the beginning. For this purpose, Jesus was manifested, that he might destroy the works of the devil. You said in your word (Romans 10:13 KJV) that whosoever shall call on the name of the Lord shall be saved. I call upon Jesus right now, I believe he died on the cross for my sins, so that I might have eternal life. I believe he was raised on the third day, and is alive seated at the right hand of God right now. I confess that I am a sinner, and I repent of my sins and I ask you to forgive me. Lord Jesus, come into my heart, and live your life in me and through me. I give myself totally and completely to you. Father God, from this moment on, I now confess Jesus as my Lord and Savior. Jesus use my life as a living testimony, as I use my life to serve you. In Jesus' name, Amen.

Now that you have accepted salvation, it is important for you to join and get involved in a bible based church.

CONTACT

I hope this book has blessed and encouraged you. If you would like to contact Min. Jennifer, please send an e-mail to marvellousandmoreministries@gmail.com